INSIDE THE NFL

NEW ENGLAND PATRIOTS

by Charlie Beattie

Abdo & Daughters
MIDDLE GRADE NONFICTION

An imprint of Abdo Publishing
abdobooks.com

ABDOBOOKS.COM

Published by Abdo Publishing, a division of ABDO, PO Box 398166, Minneapolis, Minnesota 55439.

Printed in China.
052025
092025

Cover Photos: Bryan Bennett/Getty Images Sport/Getty Images (Drake Maye); Jim Davis/Boston Globe/Getty Images (Tom Brady)
Interior Photos: Harry How/Getty Images Sport/Getty Images, 4-5; Elsa/Getty Images Sport/Getty Images, 7, 8; Maddie Meyer/Getty Images Sport/Getty Images, 9, 59; Chuck Burton/AP Images, 10; David E. Klutho/Sports Illustrated/Getty Images, 11; Abdo Publishing, 12-13, 58; Focus on Sport/Getty Images, 14-15; Focus on Sport/Getty Images Sport/Getty Images, 17, 47, 60 (bottom left); RZ/AP Images, 18; Donald Preston/Boston Globe/Getty Images, 19; Al Messerschmidt Archive/AP Images, 20, 24-25, 34-35; AP Images, 21, 27; Arthur Anderson/Getty Images Sport/Getty Images, 22; Winslow Townson/AP Images for Panini/AP Images, 23; Rick Stewart/Getty Images Sport/Getty Images, 26; Doug Mills/AP Images, 29; Mark Duncan/AP Images, 30; Elaine Thompson/AP Images, 31, 60 (top); Mitchell Layton/Getty Images Sport/Getty Images, 33; Matthew J. Lee/Boston Globe/Getty Images, 36; Kathy Willens/AP Images, 37, 52, 61 (top); Tom DiPace/AP Images, 38; Ronald C. Modra/Getty Images Sport/Getty Images, 40; Jim Davis/Boston Globe/Getty Images, 41, 61 (bottom left); Brian Bahr/Getty Images Sport/Getty Images, 42; Nancy Lane/MediaNews Group/Boston Herald/Getty Images, 43; Winslow Townson/AP Images, 45; Bill Kostroun/AP Images, 46; Damian Strohmeyer/AP Images, 48-49, 57, 60 (bottom right), 63; Charlie Riedel/AP Images, 50, 56, 61 (bottom right); Gregory Payan/AP Images, 53; Ezra Shaw/Getty Images Sport/Getty Images, 54; Paul Spinelli/AP Images, 55; Winslow Townson/Getty Images Sport/Getty Images, 59

Editor: Rebecca Higgins
Series Designer: Laura Graphenteen
Production Designer: Laura Kuchar

Library of Congress Control Number: 2024948464

Publisher's Cataloging-in-Publication Data

Names: Beattie, Charlie, author.
Title: New England Patriots / by Charlie Beattie
Description: Minneapolis, Minnesota: Abdo Publishing, 2026 | Series: Inside the NFL | Includes online resources and index.
Identifiers: ISBN 9781098296834 (lib. bdg.) | ISBN 9798384919353 (ebook)
Subjects: LCSH: New England Patriots (Football team)--Juvenile literature. | National Football League--Juvenile literature. | Football teams--Juvenile literature. | American football--Juvenile literature.
Classification: DDC 796.33264--dc23

CONTENTS

New England Patriots wide receiver Julian Edelman catches a pass during Super Bowl LIII.

CHAPTER 1

MASTER OF DEFENSE

The New England Patriots had won five Super Bowls between the 2001 and 2016 seasons. Only the Los Angeles Rams stood in the way of a record-tying sixth championship at Super Bowl LIII on February 3, 2019. But the Patriots faced a daunting challenge. Los Angeles had one of the most potent offenses in the National Football League (NFL) that season. It was up to the Patriots and their head coach, Bill Belichick, to find a way to stop the Rams.

The Patriots did just that in the first quarter. Over two possessions, the Rams moved a total of 24 yards. They gained only a single first down. However, the Rams defense shut down the Patriots too. With the score still 0–0, the Rams tried again early in the second quarter. Lining up at their own 9-yard line, Los Angeles faced third-and-seven.

Rams quarterback Jared Goff took the snap and dropped back to pass. Seeing a receiver about to cut through the middle, Goff sent a pass that way. It never got there. New England defensive end John Simon shot a hand up and knocked the ball down. For the third time in three possessions, the Rams were forced to punt. Belichick's plan was working to perfection.

STOPPING THE RAMS

Behind Goff, the Rams had averaged nearly 33 points per game during the 2018 season. Only one team had scored more points. The Rams had a solid running game along with the talented receiving corps of Robert Woods and Brandin Cooks. That created the kind of challenge Belichick thrived on solving.

Belichick's reputation as a defensive genius began when he was an assistant coach during the 1980s. That reputation only grew after he took over as the Patriots' head coach in 2000. Belichick's teams became known for their innovative defenses, as Belichick moved players around in creative ways to create havoc for opponents. With Belichick on the sideline and quarterback Tom Brady behind center, the Patriots had played in eight Super Bowls and won five of them.

Belichick knew he would have to be at his coaching best to beat the Rams and win another championship. He had just the plan in mind. To stop the run, the coach often pushed six linemen to the line of scrimmage. On passing plays, the two Patriots defenders at the end of the line would drop back and cover receivers out of the backfield. The scheme worked. Going into halftime, the Rams still hadn't advanced past the New England 42-yard line. There was one problem, however: The Patriots' offense hadn't done much either. New England entered the second half leading just 3–0.

Goff and the Rams finally got something going on their third possession after halftime. Over six plays, they moved 48 yards to the New England 29-yard line. It was their first time being within 30 yards of the end zone.

On first down, Cooks got wide-open in the Patriots' end zone. But just as Goff's pass reached Cooks's hands, Patriots defensive back Jason McCourty knocked the ball from the receiver's grip.

Defensive end Jason McCourty's (30) pass breakup in the third quarter was a key play for New England in Super Bowl LIII.

A pair of New England defenders sack Rams quarterback Jared Goff during Super Bowl LIII.

Los Angeles managed to gain 3 yards on a short pass on second down. On third down, the Patriots sacked Goff again. Just like that, the Rams' best chance yet fizzled out. They settled for a field goal to tie the game 3–3.

FINDING THE END ZONE

The Patriots needed to make something happen on offense. They finally did midway through the fourth quarter. On second-and-three from the Rams' 31, Brady dropped back and lobbed a pass down the left sideline. Three Rams defenders blanketed Rob Gronkowski.

Patriots tight end Rob Gronkowski makes his important catch in the fourth quarter against the Rams.

But the big Patriots tight end lunged to catch the pass before coming down at the 2-yard line. It was the first time either team had entered the opponent's red zone all game. On the next play, New England running back Sony Michel punched the ball over the goal line for a 10–3 lead.

The Rams got the ball back and put together their best drive of the game. Goff completed three passes to move the ball to the New England 27-yard line. On first down, the young quarterback lobbed a pass into the end zone for Cooks. New England safety Duron Harmon raced over to knock the ball free. Goff tried again on the next play. The Patriots blitzed, forcing Goff to lob the ball up.

Patriots cornerback Stephon Gilmore leaps to make an interception in the fourth quarter of Super Bowl LIII.

New England cornerback Stephon Gilmore leaped and pulled the ball into his chest at the 4-yard line for a huge interception.

With a little more than four minutes remaining, New England began handing the ball off to Michel. Seven of the next eight plays went to the running back, with backfield partner Rex Burkhead taking the other. Eating up more than three minutes off the clock, the backs drove New England to the Rams' 24. With 1:16 left, Patriots kicker Stephen Gostkowski lined up for a 41-yard field goal. As the

LOW SCORING

Super Bowl LIII was the lowest scoring Super Bowl in history. The closest comparison was Super Bowl III in January 1969, when the New York Jets beat the Baltimore Colts 16-7. New England's 13 points were the fewest ever for a Super Bowl-winning team.

Mercedes-Benz Stadium in Atlanta celebrates the Patriots winning Super Bowl LIII.

ball spun through the uprights, New England's players pumped their fists on the sideline.

When the Rams' last possession fizzled out, the Patriots secured a 13–3 win and their sixth Super Bowl title. Facing one of the league's best offenses, New England had allowed only 260 total yards. The Patriots became the first team to hold a Super Bowl opponent without a touchdown in almost 50 years, since the Dallas Cowboys did so in Super Bowl VI after the 1971 season.

After the game, Rams head coach Sean McVay told reporters he was surprised by the Patriots' tough defense. "They did a great job. It was a great game plan," he said. "There is no other way to say it, but I got outcoached." Many other NFL coaches experienced the same feeling during the Patriots' two decades of dominance.

> **"THEY DID A GREAT JOB. IT WAS A GREAT GAME PLAN. THERE IS NO OTHER WAY TO SAY IT, BUT I GOT OUTCOACHED."**
>
> —RAMS HEAD COACH SEAN MCVAY

NFL TEAMS MAP

NFC EAST

 DALLAS COWBOYS

 NEW YORK GIANTS

 PHILADELPHIA EAGLES

 WASHINGTON COMMANDERS

NFC WEST

 ARIZONA CARDINALS

 LOS ANGELES RAMS

 SAN FRANCISCO 49ERS

 SEATTLE SEAHAWKS

NFC NORTH

 CHICAGO BEARS

 DETROIT LIONS

 GREEN BAY PACKERS

 MINNESOTA VIKINGS

NFC SOUTH

 ATLANTA FALCONS

 CAROLINA PANTHERS

 NEW ORLEANS SAINTS

 TAMPA BAY BUCCANEERS

AFC

AFC EAST

- BUFFALO BILLS
- MIAMI DOLPHINS
- NEW ENGLAND PATRIOTS
- NEW YORK JETS

AFC WEST

- DENVER BRONCOS
- KANSAS CITY CHIEFS
- LAS VEGAS RAIDERS
- LOS ANGELES CHARGERS

AFC NORTH

- BALTIMORE RAVENS
-  CINCINNATI BENGALS
-  CLEVELAND BROWNS
-  PITTSBURGH STEELERS

AFC SOUTH

-  HOUSTON TEXANS
- INDIANAPOLIS COLTS
-  JACKSONVILLE JAGUARS
-  TENNESSEE TITANS

Patriots owner Billy Sullivan greets fans in 1984.

CHAPTER 2

BOSTON BEGINNINGS

In the 1950s, businessman Billy Sullivan tried to get an NFL team for his hometown of Boston. The league said no. Since the NFL's founding in 1920, five teams had already tried to make a go of it in the city. All five failed. The NFL wasn't eager to make it six. Instead, Sullivan joined up with would-be owners from other cities to create the American Football League (AFL).

The AFL began in 1960 with eight teams. Sullivan's Boston Patriots were one of the last franchises to officially join the league. And when the games started, the Patriots struggled. Under the direction of head coach Lou Saban, Boston lost the first game in league history 13–10 to the Denver Broncos. With the worst offense in the league, the Patriots went on to finish 5–9.

PLAYING FOR THE CROWN

After a 2–3 start in 1961, Saban was fired. Assistant Mike Holovak took over the top role and quickly turned the team around. He benched starting quarterback Butch Songin in favor of Babe Parilli. Boston's offense took off. Parilli was the AFL's most accurate passer that season and threw for 13 touchdowns. Gino Cappelletti became one of his favorite targets and led the team in receptions and receiving yards.

One of the AFL's most versatile players, Cappelletti was also the team's kicker and a great defensive player. In 1960, he had recorded four interceptions while playing safety on defense. Behind his continued well-rounded play in 1961, the Patriots finished 9–4–1. At the time, the AFL's two division champions met for the league title. Though Boston fell shy of the AFL title game, the team was putting together a talented roster. Defensive end Larry Eisenhauer anchored the defense. The team also drafted linebacker Nick Buoniconti in 1962. The sturdy linebacker was just starting his Hall of Fame career.

Those players led the Patriots to a 7–6–1 record in 1963, tying them with the Buffalo Bills atop the AFL's East Division. The two teams met for a one-game playoff at War Memorial Stadium in Buffalo. The winner would reach the league's championship game.

Parilli had a great game against the Bills. The 33-year-old quarterback hooked up with bruising fullback Larry Garron on a 59-yard touchdown pass in the first quarter. In the first half, Cappelletti booted three field goals as the Patriots took a 16–0 lead. Though the Patriots' normally stout defense allowed a 93-yard

Kicker Gino Cappelletti, *right*, scored 1,130 points with the Boston Patriots.

touchdown pass in the third quarter, the Patriots shut down Buffalo the rest of the way. Parilli threw a 17-yard touchdown pass to Garron in the fourth quarter, and Cappelletti's fourth field goal sealed a 26–8 win.

The championship game against San Diego wasn't nearly as exciting for Boston fans. Though Garron sprinted 7 yards for a first-quarter touchdown, the Patriots produced few highlights. San Diego rolled to a 51–10 victory.

NEW ENGLAND'S TEAM

The Patriots won 10 games in 1964, the most in team history at that point. But they finished in second place behind the Bills. Though Boston fans didn't get to see anymore postseason football during the decade, they did get to watch some star players. Running back Jim Nance was one of them. He led the AFL in rushing two straight years. In 1966, Nance set an AFL record with 1,458 yards. He was the league's Most Valuable Player (MVP) that year, but the Patriots finished 8–4–2 and missed the postseason again.

Boston didn't have a winning record for the rest of the decade, but the AFL was thriving. The NFL was worried enough about the upstart league that it decided to join forces with the AFL. The leagues agreed to have their winners meet in a championship game. The matchup started after the 1966 season. However, the leagues officially merged under the NFL name in 1970. This championship later became known as the Super Bowl.

Patriots running back Jim Nance (35) dives over the Buffalo Bills' defense for a touchdown.

The AFL-NFL merger presented a problem for Boston. As part of the deal, all NFL teams were required to play in stadiums that held at least 50,000 fans. The Patriots had four homes during the 1960s. Three were local college stadiums. The fourth was Fenway Park, home of the Red Sox baseball team. None of the stadiums were up to the NFL's new standard.

There also wasn't enough available land in Boston to build a new stadium. Sullivan secured a plot 30 miles (48 km) south of the city in Foxborough. It was far enough away from Boston that the name "Boston Patriots" no longer fit. When the new field, named Schaefer Stadium, opened in 1971, the team was officially renamed the New England Patriots.

Schaefer Stadium was the Patriots' home until 2002. The venue was also called Sullivan Stadium and Foxboro Stadium.

REBUILDING

Between 1970 and 1972, the Patriots finished a combined 11–31. In the 1973 draft, New England had three picks in the first round. The team selected offensive lineman John Hannah, running back Sam Cunningham, and receiver Darryl Stingley. All three became key pieces of New England's team. Hannah, considered one of the best guards in league history, made 10 straight All-Pro teams in a Hall of Fame career. Cunningham became the Patriots' all-time leading rusher. Stingley, meanwhile, developed into the team's top receiver.

New England offensive lineman John Hannah missed only five of a possible 191 games in his career due to injuries.

Receiver Darryl Stingley (84) makes a catch against the Oakland Raiders in the divisional playoffs after the 1976 season.

Under fourth-year head coach Chuck Fairbanks, the Patriots finally turned the corner in 1976. Cunningham and second-year quarterback Steve Grogan guided New England to the league's second-highest scoring offense. On defense, rookie cornerback Mike Haynes had a team-high eight interceptions and won the Defensive Rookie of the Year Award. With an 11–3 record, the Patriots finished second in the American Football Conference (AFC) East Division and reached the playoffs.

Seeking their first postseason victory in 13 years, the Patriots traveled to Oakland to face the powerhouse Raiders in the divisional round. The Patriots held a 21–17 lead late in the fourth quarter, but Oakland had the ball.

On third down, Raiders quarterback Ken Stabler dropped back and threw a deep pass that fell incomplete. However, just

A controversial penalty by Ray Hamilton (71) was a key moment in the Patriots' 1976 playoff game against the Oakland Raiders.

after the pass, New England defensive lineman Ray "Sugar Bear" Hamilton slammed into Stabler. The officials called Hamilton for a controversial roughing-the-passer penalty. Given 15 yards, a first down, and new life, the Raiders drove for the winning score as New England lost 24–21.

CONTROVERSY

In a 1978 preseason matchup against the Raiders, Stingley lunged for a pass over the middle of the field. Oakland safety Jack Tatum drilled the defenseless receiver. The hit paralyzed Stingley and ended his career. Though Tatum's hit was legal at the time, it led to rule changes designed to penalize violent hits on defenseless players. Without their top pass catcher, the Patriots turned to their ground game. Behind a league record 3,165 rushing yards, New England put together its best season since joining the NFL. Cunningham led the way with 798 rushing yards, and three other players, including Grogan, rushed for more than 500 yards. With an 11–5 record, the Patriots won their first division title in 15 years.

However, the season ended in chaos. Before the Patriots' last regular-season game, Fairbanks announced he would leave after the season to coach the team at the University of Colorado. Frustrated, Sullivan didn't allow Fairbanks to coach in the finale. But after a brutal 23–3 loss to the Miami Dolphins, Sullivan changed his mind and reinstated Fairbanks before the Patriots' playoff matchup against the Houston Oilers. It was too little too late. Houston crushed the disorganized Patriots 31–14. New England didn't reach the playoffs again in the 1970s.

PAT PATRIOT

The Patriots' original logo came from an unlikely source. When the team was named, local newspaper cartoonist Phil Bissell created a cartoon of a Revolutionary War (1775–1783) minuteman about to snap a football. Team owner Billy Sullivan liked the image, and paid Bissell $100 for it. Bissell's cartoon soldier became "Pat Patriot." The team used that logo until it redesigned its uniforms in 1993.

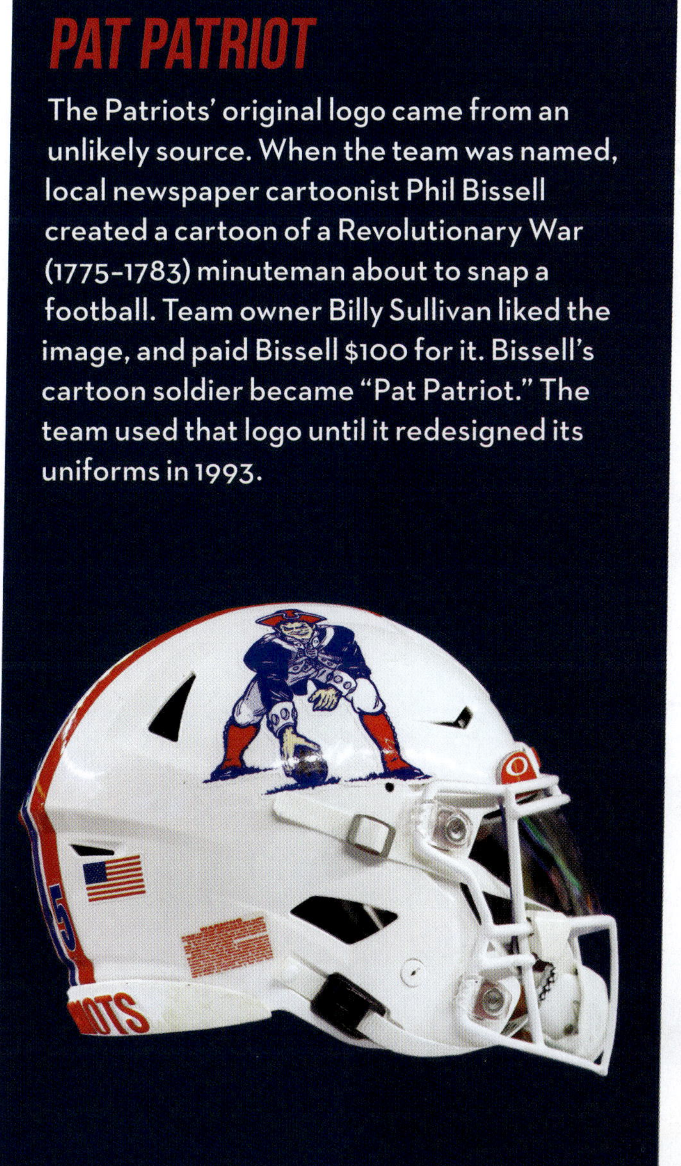

Patriots linebacker Andre Tippett (56) was named to the All-Pro team twice in his NFL career.

CHAPTER 3

SUPER BOWL BOUND

THE PATRIOTS RETURNED TO THE PLAYOFFS AFTER A STRIKE-SHORTENED 1982 season but fell 28–13 to the Miami Dolphins. That proved to be the high point of the early 1980s. However, the team was once again stockpiling talented players. In 1982, the team selected Andre Tippett in the second round of the draft. Over his next 11 seasons, the speedy linebacker became the first Patriots player to record 100 sacks. He was eventually enshrined in the Hall of Fame.

The Patriots had another impactful draft in 1983. New England picked quarterback Tony Eason, running back Craig James, and defensive back Ronnie Lippett. A year later, the Patriots drafted receiver Irving Fryar to pair with veteran Stanley Morgan. When the team brought in coach Raymond Berry midway through the 1984 season,

Patriots quarterback Steve Grogan is sacked by a pair of Bears defenders in Super Bowl XX.

things finally started to click. Though the Patriots missed the playoffs that year, they came back in 1985 ready to contend.

Eason and veteran Steve Grogan shared the quarterback job. But James led the way on offense, rushing for more than 1,200 yards. Fryar and Morgan had a combined total of 12 touchdown catches. But New England's real strength was its defense. Tippett recorded 16 1/2 sacks while Lippett picked off three passes. The Patriots held opponents to 18.1 points per game while finishing 11–5.

With the third-best record in the AFC East, New England opened the playoffs on the road against the rival New York Jets. Behind four field goals by kicker Tony Franklin, New England marched on to a 26–14 win. It was the team's first postseason win in two decades.

In January 1986, the Patriots carry head coach Raymond Berry off the field after beating the Miami Dolphins in the AFC Championship Game.

After beating the Los Angeles Raiders in the divisional round, New England went to Miami to play the defending AFC-champion Dolphins. The winner would earn a spot in the Super Bowl. The Patriots had lost 18 consecutive games at Miami's vaunted Orange Bowl. This time New England's defense forced six turnovers. Eason capitalized with three touchdown passes in a 31–14 victory. The streak was over, and the Patriots were on their way to the Super Bowl.

As a reward, New England faced one of the all-time great teams in Super Bowl XX. Behind their dominant defense, the Chicago Bears had lost just once all season. At the Super Bowl in New Orleans, Chicago stuffed the Patriots, holding New England

"IT WAS LIKE TRYING TO BEAT BACK THE TIDE WITH A BROOM."

—RON WOOTEN

to just 123 yards. The Bears sacked the Patriots' quarterback duo seven times in a crushing 46–10 win. After the game, Patriots guard Ron Wooten described blocking the Bears: "It was like trying to beat back the tide with a broom."

OWNERSHIP STRUGGLES

The Patriots followed up their Super Bowl run with a division title in 1986 but lost their playoff opener. While the team seemed strong on the field, things were becoming ugly behind the scenes. Facing bankruptcy, longtime owner Billy Sullivan put the team up for sale.

In 1988, entrepreneur Victor Kiam bought the Patriots, while businessman Robert Kraft purchased the stadium. Under the new arrangement, Kraft made money on home games from parking and concessions. Kiam earned money from ticket sales and the NFL's television deal. It was an unusual setup, and it turned the Patriots into a dysfunctional team.

THE KING OF POP SINKS THE PATS

In 1984, Patriots owner Billy Sullivan tried to cash in by investing in pop superstar Michael Jackson. Sullivan helped promote Jackson's "Victory" tour that year, which was supposed to be a big success. But the tour lost huge amounts of money. Sullivan took such a big financial hit that he could no longer afford the Patriots.

Before long Kiam was losing money, and the team couldn't afford to pay its players' high salaries. Unable to put a good team on the field, the Patriots began dropping in the standings. New England bottomed out in 1990 by finishing 1–15. Two years later, Kiam sold the Patriots to a businessman from St. Louis named James Orthwein. Many fans feared that the new owner would move the Patriots to his home city, which had just lost the Cardinals to Arizona.

A NEW BEGINNING

Instead of moving the team, Orthwein made two moves that helped turn New England around. First, he hired Bill Parcells as head coach in 1993. The tough, disciplined Parcells was considered one of the league's best coaches. He had coached the New York Giants from 1983 to 1990 and led them to a pair of Super Bowl wins.

Also in 1993, the Patriots had the first pick in the NFL Draft. They selected quarterback Drew Bledsoe. Bledsoe was a typical NFL quarterback for the time at 6 feet, 5 inches tall. While he wasn't very mobile, he was able to stand in the pocket and drop strong, accurate passes all over the field. By his second season, Bledsoe led the NFL with 400 completions and an NFL-record 691 pass attempts. His phenomenal play carried New England to a 10–6 record and back to the playoffs.

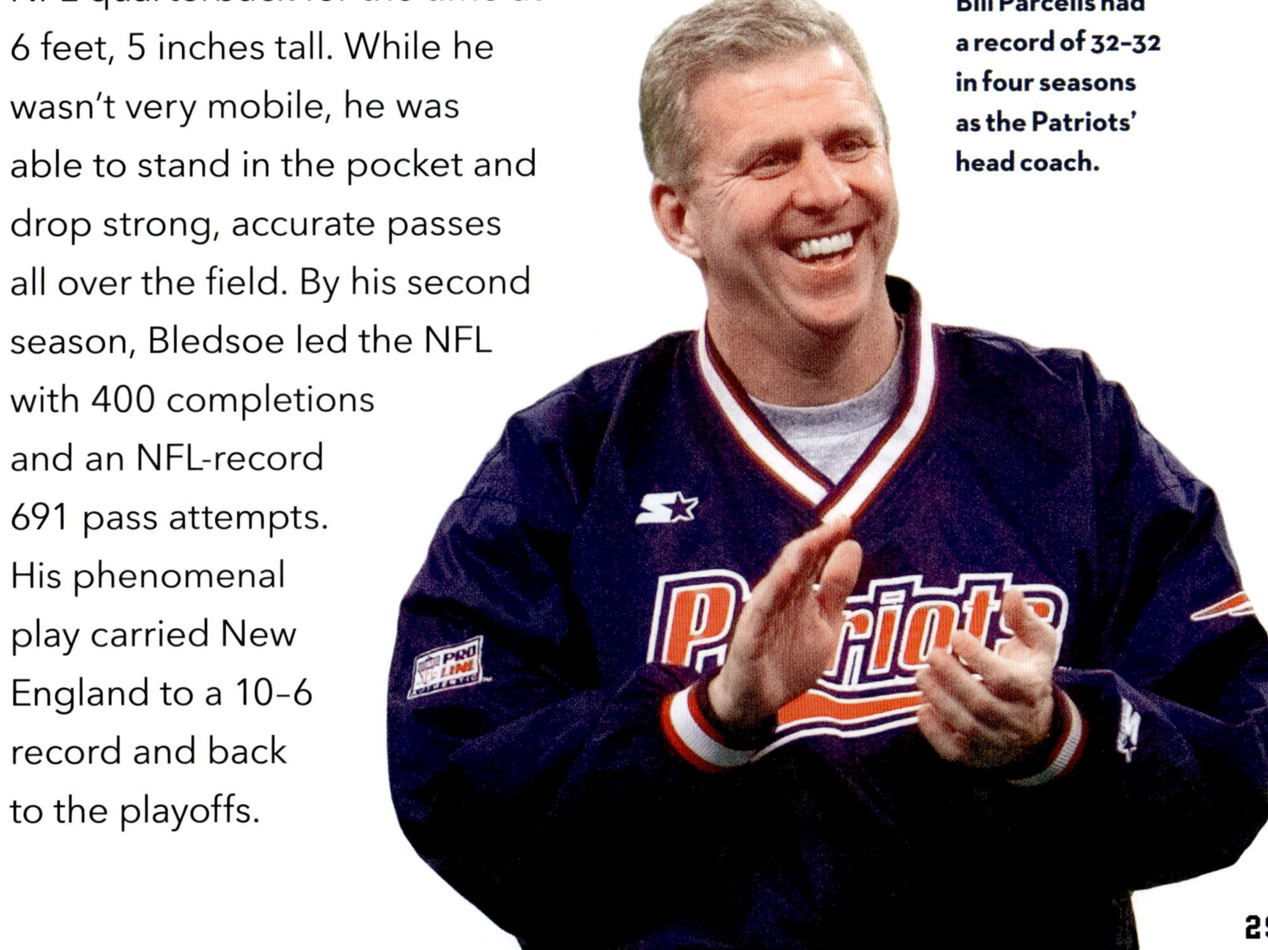

Bill Parcells had a record of 32–32 in four seasons as the Patriots' head coach.

However, the Patriots fell 20–13 to the Cleveland Browns in the wild-card round.

The Browns' coach in that game was Bill Belichick. A year later, Cleveland fired him, and Belichick joined Parcells as New England's assistant head coach. He coached the Patriots' defensive backs. In 1996, the team's defense rapidly improved. With Bledsoe and star running back Curtis Martin leading one of the NFL's best offenses, the Patriots shot up the standings. After losing their first two games, the Patriots finished the season 11–3. New England then didn't allow a single touchdown in two playoff games as it beat the Pittsburgh Steelers 28–3 and the Jacksonville Jaguars 20–6.

Quarterback Drew Bledsoe throws a pass in a playoff game against the Cleveland Browns after the 1994 season.

Just three years after being one of the worst teams in the league, the Patriots returned to the Super Bowl. However, once again, they were a heavy underdog, this time to the Green Bay Packers.

The Patriots kept Super Bowl XXXI close, but they kept giving up big plays. In the first half, Green Bay scored on touchdown passes of 54 and 81 yards. A 99-yard kickoff return by the

Running back Curtis Martin rushed for 42 yards and a touchdown on 11 carries in Super Bowl XXXI against the Green Bay Packers on January 26, 1997.

Packers' Desmond Howard in the third quarter sealed the Patriots' 35–21 defeat.

COACHING CAROUSEL

After owning the Patriots for two years, Orthwein sold the team to Kraft in 1994. Parcells had reached an agreement with the new owner. The coach could leave the Patriots after the 1996 season, but if he did, he was not allowed to coach another NFL team in 1997. After the Super Bowl loss to Green Bay, Parcells did leave the Patriots. And when Parcells tried to take the head coaching job with the rival New York Jets, Kraft refused to let him.

The Jets responded by hiring Belichick as head coach instead. They then hired Parcells as a consultant. However, the title was simply a way to work around Parcells's earlier deal with Kraft. The Patriots were upset and demanded the NFL punish the Jets for breaking Kraft's agreement with Parcells.

League commissioner Paul Tagliabue stepped in and worked out a deal. Ultimately the Patriots got some of the Jets' upcoming draft picks in exchange for Parcells. Meanwhile, Belichick stayed with Parcells and became his defensive coordinator in New York.

The Patriots moved on with new coach Pete Carroll, and they remained competitive. New England reached the playoffs after the 1997 and 1998 seasons. Then the team finished 8–8 and was out of the postseason in 1999. After the season, Carroll was fired.

Meanwhile, down in New York, Parcells retired from the Jets after the 1999 season. On January 3, 2000, New York announced that Belichick was set to become its new head coach. The next day,

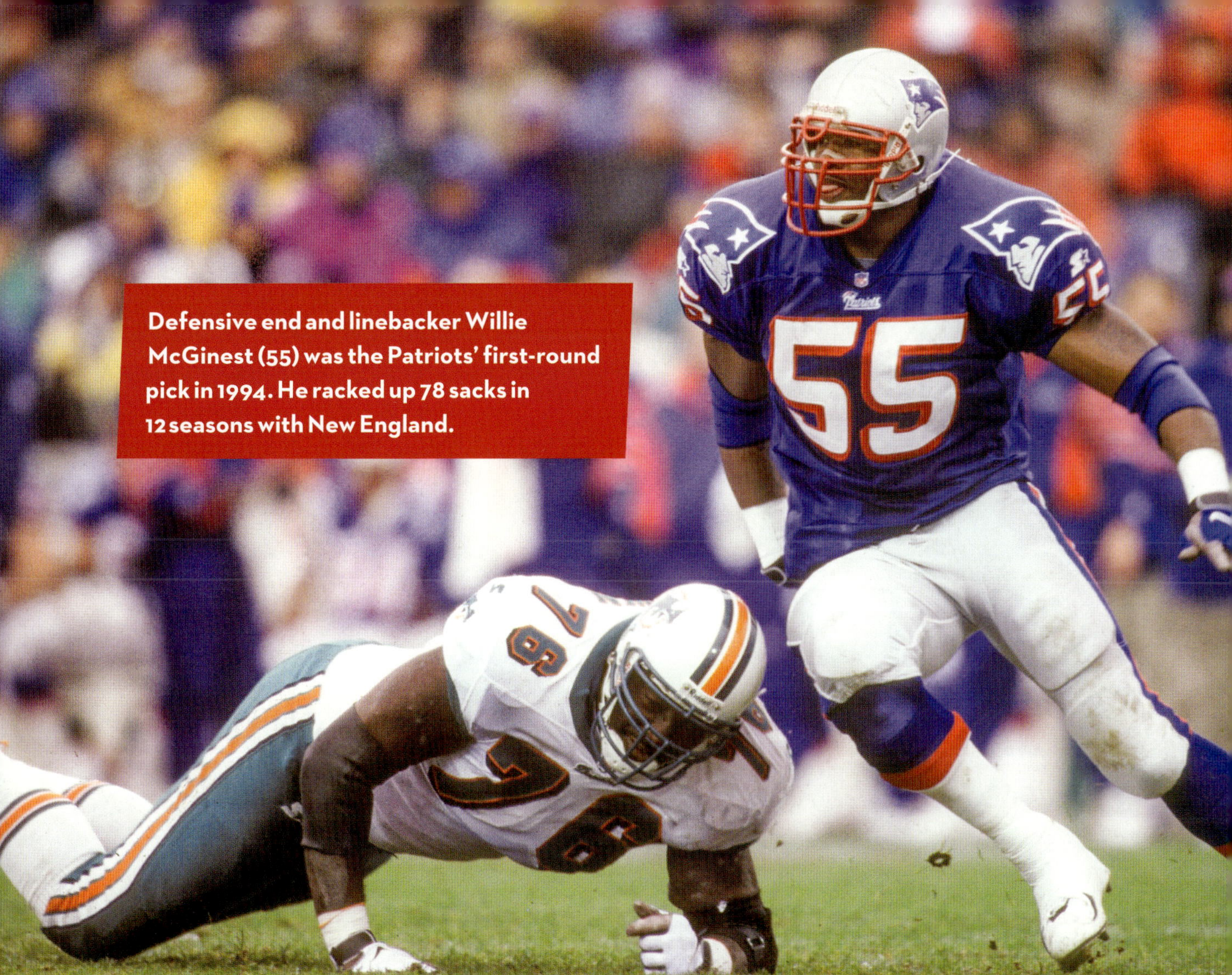
Defensive end and linebacker Willie McGinest (55) was the Patriots' first-round pick in 1994. He racked up 78 sacks in 12 seasons with New England.

Belichick called a press conference and said that he had changed his mind. Kraft immediately hired Belichick to coach New England. This time, the Jets complained, and the NFL forced the Patriots to give up a handful of draft choices to New York.

That coaching drama captured the attention of football fans everywhere. Fewer took notice months later when the Patriots made their second sixth-round pick in the NFL Draft. With the 199th selection, New England added Michigan quarterback Tom Brady. Few believed he had what it took to become a starter in the NFL. Soon Brady would show he could be much more than that.

Drew Bledsoe, *left*, talks strategy with fellow Patriots quarterback Tom Brady during a 2001 game.

CHAPTER 4

FROM UNDERDOGS TO DYNASTY

Drew Bledsoe rolled to his right, but all his receivers were covered. The veteran quarterback took off toward the sideline. It was Week 2 of the 2001 season, and the Patriots were already 0–1. Now they trailed the New York Jets 10–3 with just over five minutes to go.

As Bledsoe reached the sideline, Jets linebacker Mo Lewis hammered the Patriots' quarterback. Bledsoe left the game injured, and New England punted. Bledsoe returned for the next series. But on the game's final series, Tom Brady ran onto the field. Brady had thrown only three passes in his NFL career. He nearly led a game-tying drive in the final seconds. However, the Patriots fell short, losing 10–3. Then the team announced Bledsoe would miss the next several weeks. Another losing season appeared on its way.

Instead, Brady stepped in and played well. The young signal-caller was a tough competitor and cool under pressure. He led three fourth-quarter comebacks on the way to an 11–3 record over the rest of the season.

New England receiver David Patten spikes the ball after scoring a touchdown against the Pittsburgh Steelers in the AFC Championship Game after the 2001 season.

GOING FOR THE WIN

The Patriots held off the Oakland Raiders in a tight playoff game. That set up an AFC title game showdown with the Pittsburgh Steelers. Just before halftime, Brady left the game with an injury. In his place, Bledsoe guided the team to a 24–17 win and a trip back to the Super Bowl. Now the question was which quarterback should start against the St. Louis Rams in Super Bowl XXXVI.

The team ultimately went with Brady. But few observers thought the decision would matter. With an exceptional offense, the Rams were heavy favorites. But when the game started, it was Belichick's defense that shined first.

The Patriots' offense struggled to move the ball. Then, in the second quarter, New England cornerback Ty Law grabbed an interception and sprinted for a 47-yard touchdown. The Patriots entered the fourth quarter up 17–3. Finally, the Rams' offense woke up. The Rams scored twice to tie the game with just over one minute remaining.

New England took over on its 17-yard line with 1:21 to play and no timeouts. It was a difficult situation for any quarterback. Any mistake could give the Rams an easy score and the Super Bowl title.

Patriots cornerback Ty Law, *left*, hauls in an interception before returning it 47 yards for a touchdown in the second quarter of Super Bowl XXXVI.

Brady throws a pass against the St. Louis Rams in Super Bowl XXXVI.

Many people watching, including legendary broadcaster John Madden, suggested that the Patriots should kneel the clock out and try to win the game in overtime instead of trying to aggressively move the ball downfield.

"WITH A QUARTERBACK LIKE BRADY, GOING FOR THE WIN IS NOT THAT DANGEROUS, BECAUSE HE'S NOT GOING TO MAKE A MISTAKE."

—BILL BELICHICK

Belichick opted to go for the win. He trusted his young star. "With a quarterback like Brady, going for the win is not that dangerous, because he's not going to make a mistake," Belichick said later. Brady calmly guided the Patriots to the St. Louis 30-yard line with eight seconds remaining. Patriots kicker Adam Vinatieri had already booted one overtime winner in these playoffs. With time expiring in the Super Bowl, Vinatieri split the uprights again. His 48-yard kick delivered New England its first championship.

BACK-TO-BACK

The Patriots' Super Bowl win was considered a huge upset. And when New England failed to make the playoffs in 2002, many wrote off the 2001 team as a fluke. The start to the 2003 season did little to change that thinking.

New England opened on the road against the Buffalo Bills. Brady played terribly and was eventually benched after throwing four interceptions. To make matters worse, Bledsoe had taken over as the Bills' quarterback. After Bledsoe led a 31–0 romp against his former team, many wondered whether the Patriots had kept the wrong quarterback.

Brady quickly quieted any concerns. He and the Patriots bounced back from the season-opening loss to go 14–1 the rest of the way. The young quarterback had plenty of help from the league's best defense. On the defensive line, Willie McGinest and Richard Seymour stuffed opposing runners. Behind them

THE TUCK RULE

A heavy snowstorm wreaked havoc in Foxborough as the New England Patriots hosted the Oakland Raiders for a playoff game on January 19, 2002. Late in regulation, the Patriots trailed 13–10 but were driving. Brady dropped back to pass, but his arm was hit and the ball came loose. Oakland recovered what was seemingly a game-clinching fumble. However, the officials said that Brady was "tucking" the ball toward his body and that the play was actually an incomplete pass. Five plays later, New England kicker Adam Vinatieri tied the game. New England won "the Tuck Rule" game in overtime on its way to the Super Bowl.

were hard-hitting linebacker Tedy Bruschi and safety Rodney Harrison. Law was one of the NFL's best cornerbacks. Behind those stars, New England posted three shutouts while holding opponents to 14.9 points per game.

Linebacker Tedy Bruschi played 13 seasons with the Patriots and was named to the Pro Bowl in 2004.

The Patriots carried their momentum all the way to Super Bowl XXXVIII against the Carolina Panthers. Through three quarters, the defenses dominated. New England held a slim 14–10 lead. The teams then combined for 37 points in a wild fourth quarter.

With 1:08 left, the Panthers tied the game 29–29. Then New England caught a huge break. Carolina kicker John Kasay booted his kickoff out of bounds, which gave the Patriots the ball at the 40-yard line. With such a good starting spot, Brady once again guided his team into field goal position. With four seconds left, Vinatieri delivered from 41 yards. He secured a 32–29 lead and another Super Bowl win for New England.

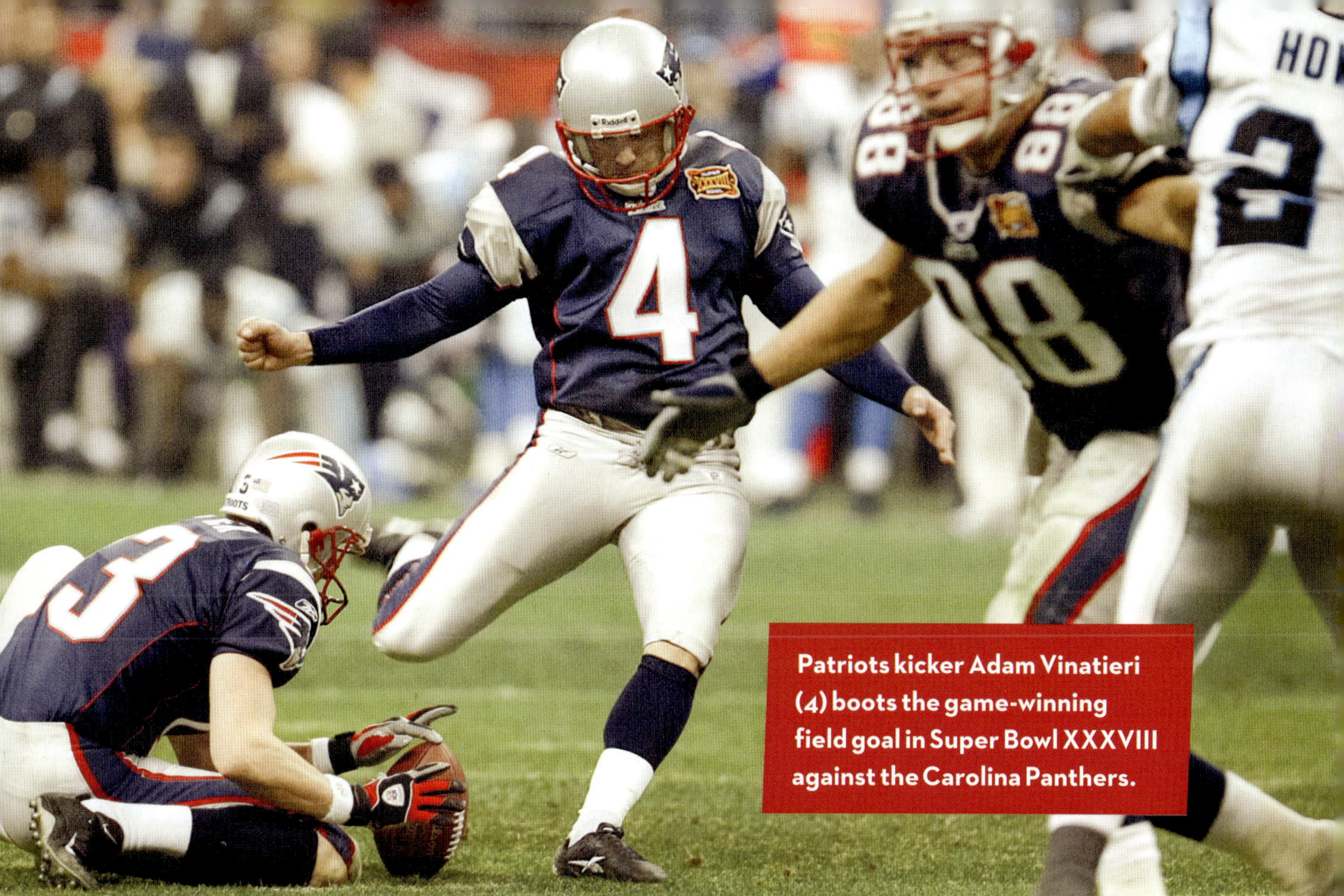

Patriots kicker Adam Vinatieri (4) boots the game-winning field goal in Super Bowl XXXVIII against the Carolina Panthers.

The second Super Bowl victory erased doubts about Brady or the Patriots. Entering the 2004 season, the team had won 15 straight games. Brady had developed a reputation as a quarterback who could always come through in the fourth quarter. After starting the 2004 season 6–0, New England had won an NFL-record 21 straight games. The Patriots finished the season 14–2 again. Then they routed the Indianapolis Colts and the Pittsburgh Steelers in the playoffs to set up a Super Bowl matchup against the Philadelphia Eagles.

Brady dominated, completing 23 of 33 passes for 236 yards and a pair of touchdowns. However, the real star of the game was Harrison. The intimidating safety made 12 tackles, including one sack. He also picked off two passes. Harrison's second interception, with 17 seconds left, sealed New England's 24–21 victory.

SPYGATE

The Patriots had emerged as the NFL's first dynasty of the 2000s. After falling short of the Super Bowl after both the 2005 and 2006 seasons, they were contenders again in 2007. But as the season began, New England faced several controversies.

New England's Mike Vrabel catches a touchdown pass in Super Bowl XXXIX against the Philadelphia Eagles. Vrabel was a linebacker but caught touchdowns in back-to-back Super Bowls for New England.

The New York Jets had accused the Patriots of illegally videotaping their practices. That would have given New England an unfair advantage since the Patriots would know what plays the Jets were likely to call. When the league investigated these claims, it found that the Patriots had taped New York and other teams as well. A Boston newspaper reported that the Patriots had even taped the Rams before Super Bowl XXXVI. However, that story turned out to be false.

The "Spygate" scandal was one of many controversies the Patriots faced during Bill Belichick's time as head coach.

The "Spygate" scandal rocked the NFL. Some commentators suggested that New England should forfeit its Super Bowl titles. That didn't happen, but the Patriots were stripped of their first-round draft pick in 2008. Both Belichick and the team had to pay major fines. To many, the scandal cast doubt on the team's success.

ALMOST PERFECT

As the Spygate scandal unfolded in the media, the Patriots played as well as ever on the field. New England's early Super Bowl teams had been known for their stout defenses. The 2007 team was built around a record-setting offense.

Randy Moss had made a name for himself as one of the league's all-time great receivers. However, he also had a reputation for being unpredictable and selfish. So it surprised many when New England traded for him before the 2007 season. Moss didn't seem to fit in on a Patriots roster filled with overachievers who seemed to thrive in their team-first roles.

Instead, Moss proved to be a sensation. The super-athletic receiver found an instant connection with Brady, who threw a league-record 50 touchdown passes. Moss caught 23 of those scores, which was also an NFL record. And when New England held off the New York Giants 38–35 in the season finale, the Patriots were a perfect 16–0.

Since the Super Bowl era began in 1966, only the 1972 Miami Dolphins had ever gone undefeated. They went 14–0 during the regular season, then won all three playoff games to finish as league champions. When the Patriots dispatched the Jacksonville Jaguars and the San Diego Chargers in the playoffs, they were one win away from joining the Dolphins in completing a perfect season.

All New England had to do was beat the upstart Giants again in the Super Bowl. The Patriots came into the game as huge favorites, but the game turned into a close, defensive contest. The Giants' pass rush disrupted Brady all game, making it hard for him and Moss to get rolling. Still, with 2:42 left, Brady threw a 6-yard touchdown pass to Moss that put New England up 14–10. The historic victory was in sight.

In addition to his record 50 touchdown passes, Brady led the NFL with 4,806 passing yards and a 68.9 percent completion rate in 2007.

Patriots receiver Randy Moss celebrates scoring a touchdown in 2007.

Instead, the Giants marched down the field, helped by an improbable play. On third-and-five from the Giants' 44, the Patriots pressured Giants quarterback Eli Manning and came close to sacking him. He wiggled away from several Patriots and heaved a pass down the middle of the field. Giants receiver David Tyree leaped high in the air and made a 32-yard catch, pinning the ball against his helmet as Harrison tried to rip it out. A few plays later,

Manning hit Plaxico Burress for the go-ahead touchdown. With 35 seconds remaining, New York led 17–14.

Brady and the Patriots had one last chance to work some magic. However, after a season in which just about everything seemed to go right, the Patriots were finally stopped. With a stunning loss in the season's biggest game, New England fell just short of the greatest feat in NFL history.

New England safety Rodney Harrison, *right*, tries to rip the ball away from New York's David Tyree on the key play of Super Bowl XLII in February 2008.

Aside from the 2008 season, quarterback Tom Brady never missed a game due to injury in his 23-year NFL career.

CHAPTER 5

HISTORY MAKERS

HALFWAY THROUGH THE FIRST QUARTER OF THE PATRIOTS' 2008 season opener, Tom Brady fired a strike to Randy Moss down the right sideline. But as Brady threw, a Kansas City Chiefs' defender slammed into his left leg. The quarterback suffered a serious knee injury, and he was done for the season.

Without their star, the Patriots still finished 11–5 in 2008. But in the competitive AFC, that record wasn't good enough to reach the playoffs. Brady returned in 2009. In each of the next five seasons, the Patriots won the AFC East but fell short in the postseason. Their best showing came after the 2011 season when they returned to the Super Bowl for a rematch against the New York Giants. Once again, the Patriots were favored. But once again the game ended in heartbreak. New York came from behind and scored a late touchdown to steal the victory again. The Patriots then fell in the AFC title game in each of the next two seasons. Despite being consistently competitive, New England entered the 2014 season having not won a Super Bowl in 10 years.

GOAL-LINE STAND

One way the Patriots stayed strong was by frequently adapting. Instead of paying a lot to keep their stars around, the team often let top players leave and replaced them with cheaper draft picks or free agents. The only two constants in New England were Brady and head coach Bill Belichick.

In the early 2010s, Brady found two new favorite receiving targets. In 2009, the Patriots picked wide receiver Julian Edelman in the seventh round of the draft. Tight end Rob Gronkowski arrived

Rob Gronkowski caught 79 touchdowns in nine seasons with the Patriots after the team drafted him in 2010.

with more fanfare as a second-round draft pick in 2010. Together they developed into a potent duo. The undersized Edelman proved to be ultra reliable and consistent. Meanwhile, "Gronk" had a combination of speed and size that made him a matchup nightmare for defenses. After scoring, the fun-loving star celebrated by spiking the ball. That became a familiar site by 2014, as the Patriots' offensive trio was humming. Both Edelman and Gronkowski caught more than 80 passes as the Patriots finished 12–4.

New England then rolled through two playoff games to reach another Super Bowl. However, by the time the Patriots arrived in Phoenix for the big game, a new controversy had emerged. Following the AFC title game, the opposing Indianapolis Colts accused Brady of deflating the footballs he was using to a level below the NFL's standard air pressure. That way he could get a better grip on the ball in the cold weather.

The accusation hung over the Patriots as they prepared for the Super Bowl against the defending champions the Seattle Seahawks. After three quarters, New England trailed 24–14. But Brady tossed a pair of touchdown passes. The second was a 3-yard strike to Edelman to put the Patriots up 28–24 with 2:02 left.

Seattle quickly drove down the field. With 26 seconds left, the Seahawks faced second-and-goal at the New England 1. Most expected Seattle to hand the ball off to powerful running back Marshawn Lynch. Instead, quarterback Russell Wilson dropped back and fired a pass over the middle to receiver Ricardo Lockette. New England cornerback Malcolm Butler, a backup who had joined the team as an undrafted free agent, leaped in front of Lockette and

New England cornerback Malcolm Butler, *left*, makes the game-sealing interception in Super Bowl XLIX against the Seahawks after the 2014 season.

intercepted the pass at the goal line. The incredible play put the Patriots on top again.

While fans in New England celebrated the team's first championship in 10 seasons, many around the league remained furious about the scandal now dubbed "Deflategate." Many questioned whether the Patriots had won games with their talent or as a result of cheating. Brady denied the accusations. And when the NFL suspended him for the first four games of the 2015 season, he appealed. Ultimately Brady was able to play, and he led the Patriots to another NFC title game. However, he dropped the case after that, and the suspension was put into place for the start of the 2016 season.

THE COMEBACK

With Brady benched, the Patriots didn't miss a beat. Backups Jacoby Brissett and Jimmy Garoppolo led the team to a 3–1 start. Brady returned and threw 28 touchdowns and only two interceptions as the Patriots finished 14–2. Despite playing only 12 games, Brady was the runner-up for the league's Most Valuable Player (MVP) Award.

Brady was named the NFL's regular-season MVP three times in his career. He was also the Super Bowl MVP five times, including once with the Tampa Bay Buccaneers.

After cruising through a pair of playoff wins, the Patriots returned to the Super Bowl to face the Atlanta Falcons. No team had scored more than the Falcons during the regular season, and their offense clicked in the first half of Super Bowl LI in Houston. Atlanta went into the half with an 18-point lead. Another score midway through the third pushed its lead to 28–3.

In the history of the Super Bowl, no team had ever come back from more than 10 points behind. But the Patriots began to claw their way back. First, Brady connected with running back James White on a 5-yard touchdown pass late in the third quarter. After missing a field goal, New England still trailed 28–9.

The Patriots forced Atlanta to punt early in the fourth quarter, then responded with a field goal. On the Falcons' next drive, Patriots linebacker Dont'a Hightower forced a fumble at the Falcons' 25. Defensive tackle Alan Branch recovered it. Five plays later, Brady threw a 6-yard scoring pass to receiver Danny Amendola. This time, White converted the two-point conversion, cutting Atlanta's lead to 28–20.

New England got the ball back with 3:30 left and began driving down the field.

New England's Dont'a Hightower strips the ball from Atlanta quarterback Matt Ryan in the fourth quarter of Super Bowl LI following the 2016 season.

On first-and-10 from the New England 36, Brady aimed a pass down the middle for Edelman. Atlanta cornerback Robert Alford tipped the ball in the air, and Edelman had to adjust and dive for it. Two other Atlanta defenders also went for the ball. Edelman collided with them but managed to hold the ball for a juggling catch, pulling it in just inches from the ground. "It was one of the greatest catches I've ever seen. I don't know how he caught it," Brady said after the game. "I don't think [Edelman] does."

"IT WAS ONE OF THE GREATEST CATCHES I'VE EVER SEEN. I DON'T KNOW HOW HE CAUGHT IT."

—TOM BRADY

Spurred by the amazing play, the Patriots scored on a 1-yard touchdown run by White with 57 seconds left. Brady and Amendola connected on the two-point conversion to tie the game. By then,

Patriots wide receiver Julian Edelman, *right*, dives to make his incredible catch on the game-tying drive late in Super Bowl LI.

James White dives across the goal line for the winning touchdown in Super Bowl LI.

the Falcons' defense was exhausted. When New England won the coin toss to start overtime with the ball, it was over. White soon blasted his way across the goal line for a 2-yard score to complete the historic comeback and give New England its fifth Super Bowl championship. White had set a Super Bowl record with 14 receptions. After the game, Brady was named the Super Bowl MVP. It was the fourth time he had won the award.

THE END OF THE DYNASTY

The Patriots nearly won a second consecutive Super Bowl the next season. Brady threw for a Super Bowl-record 505 yards in a thrilling game against the Philadelphia Eagles. Even at 40 years old, he showed he was still one of the NFL's best quarterbacks. But it wasn't enough to win the game, as Philadelphia pulled away 41–33.

While Brady and Belichick created success on the field, their relationship began to struggle behind the scenes. Brady had begun to resent his coach's cold style. The coach also wasn't a fan of his quarterback's training methods. Brady had started working with a special trainer, hoping to play pro football until his mid-40s. Belichick wanted Brady to be working out with his teammates instead.

Still, the pair managed to lead the Patriots to another championship after the 2018 season. The Patriots defeated the Los Angeles Rams 13–3 in a defensive struggle to claim a sixth Super Bowl title. The team that had begun the 2000s without a victory in football's biggest game had tied for the most in league history.

That win over the Rams proved to be the end of the Patriots' dynasty, however. The Patriots fell in the wild-card round of the next year's playoffs. Brady left

TOM BRADY'S RECORDS

Tom Brady retired after the 2022 season having rewritten the NFL's record books. He started 333 games in his career. Brady threw for 89,214 yards and 649 touchdowns during regular-season games. Brady was known for his clutch plays. He retired as the all-time leader with 46 fourth-quarter comebacks and 58 game-winning drives.

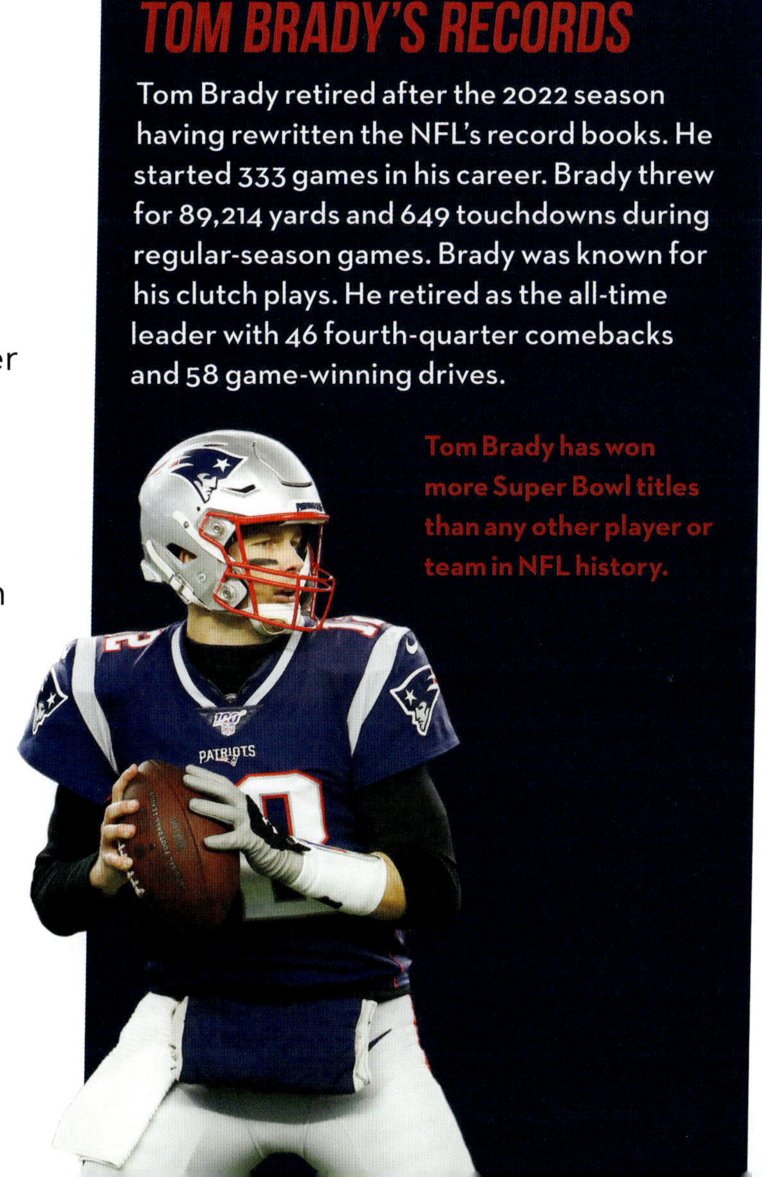

Tom Brady has won more Super Bowl titles than any other player or team in NFL history.

PATRIOTS TROPHY CASE

SUPER BOWL CHAMPIONSHIPS: 6

Super Bowl XXXVI - February 3, 2002
Super Bowl XXXVIII - February 1, 2004
Super Bowl XXXIX - February 6, 2005
Super Bowl XLIX - February 1, 2015
Super Bowl LI - February 5, 2017
Super Bowl LIII - February 3, 2019

CONFERENCE CHAMPIONSHIPS: 11

1985, 1996, 2001, 2003, 2004, 2007, 2011, 2014, 2016, 2017, 2018

DIVISION TITLES: 22

AFL East: 1963
AFC East: 1978, 1986, 1996, 1997, 2001, 2003, 2004, 2005, 2006, 2007, 2009, 2010, 2011, 2012, 2013, 2014, 2015, 2016, 2017, 2018, 2019

All stats are through the 2024 season.

XXXVI
XXXVIII
XXXIX
XLIX
LI
LIII

New England for the Tampa Bay Buccaneers in the offseason. Without him, the Patriots struggled to find a solid quarterback. Though the team returned to the playoffs after the 2021 season, the magic from years earlier was gone. After a disappointing 4–13 season in 2023, Belichick and the team parted ways. New England was officially starting over.

Patriots quarterback Drake Maye threw 15 touchdowns in 2024.

The team hired former Patriots linebacker Jerod Mayo as head coach. New England also drafted quarterback Drake Maye with the third pick in the 2024 draft. Maye impressed as a rookie, but Mayo was fired after another 4–13 finish. In his place, the Patriots hired another of their former linebackers. Mike Vrabel took the head coaching reins in January 2025 as New England continued to look for its next winning combination.

TIMELINE

The Boston Patriots are founded as one of the AFL's original teams.
1960

1964
Boston reaches the AFL title game but loses 51–10 to the San Diego Chargers on January 5.

After moving from Boston to Foxborough, Massachusetts, the team is renamed the New England Patriots
1971

1986
After finishing 11–5 in the 1985 season, the Patriots lose Super Bowl XX 46–10 to the Chicago Bears on January 26.

On January 26, the Patriots fall 35–21 to the Green Bay Packers in Super Bowl XXXI.
1997

2000
New England hires Bill Belichick as head coach and drafts Tom Brady.

The Patriots win their first Super Bowl 20–17 over the St. Louis Rams on a last-second field goal by kicker Adam Vinatieri on February 3.
2002

2004
On February 1, New England defeats the Carolina Panthers 32–29 to win Super Bowl XXXVIII.

2005
On February 6, the Patriots defeat the Philadelphia Eagles 24–21 and claim their third Super Bowl in four seasons.

2008
The Patriots reach Super Bowl XLII with an 18–0 record but are upset by the New York Giants 17–14 on February 3.

2015
On February 1, the Patriots defeat the Seattle Seahawks 28–24 in Super Bowl XLIX on Malcolm Butler's last-minute interception.

2017
The Patriots win Super Bowl LI 34–28 in overtime after rallying from 28–3 down against the Atlanta Falcons on February 5.

2019
New England wins its sixth Super Bowl by defeating the Los Angeles Rams 13–3 on February 3.

2025
Former Patriots star linebacker Mike Vrabel becomes head coach.

GLOSSARY

bankrupt–unable to pay debts.

blitz–when a linebacker or defensive back attacks the line of scrimmage to stop a run or sack the quarterback.

draft–a system that allows teams to acquire new players coming into the league.

dynasty–a team that has an extended period of success, usually winning multiple championships in the process.

franchise–an entire sports organization.

free agent–a player who is not signed to a team.

merge–join with another to create something new, such as a company, a team, or a league.

paralyze–to cause to be unable to move a part or parts of the body.

postseason–another word for playoffs; the time after the end of the regular season when teams play to determine a champion.

red zone–the area of the field between the 20-yard line and the goal line.

rookie–a professional athlete in his or her first year of competition.

sack–a tackle of the quarterback behind the line of scrimmage before he can pass the ball.

turnover–loss of the ball to the other team through an interception or fumble.

two-point conversion—an option for teams that have scored a touchdown to try a running or passing play from the 2-yard line for two points, instead of kicking for one point.

underdog—the person or team that is not expected to win.

upset—an unexpected victory by a supposedly weaker team or player.

versatile—able to perform many different roles or functions.

veteran—a player who has played for many years.

wild-card—the first round of the playoffs.

ONLINE RESOURCES

To learn more about the New England Patriots, please visit **abdobooklinks.com** or scan this QR code. These links are routinely monitored and updated to provide the most current information available.